MW01063771

Panic Ye Not!

Woodmansterne

First published in the United Kingdom in 2021 by
Portico
43 Great Ormond Street
London
WC1N 3HZ

An imprint of Pavilion Books Company Ltd

ISBN 978-1-91162-257-4

A CIP catalogue record for this book is available from the British Library.

10 9 8 7 6 5 4 3 2 1

Reproduction by Rival Colour Ltd, UK
Printed and bound by IMAK Ofset, Turkey

www.pavilionbooks.com

Panic Ye Not!

A survival guide to the middle ages

by Ian Blake

PORTICO

"Urgent news? The French defeated?"
"Nay, My Lord better! Hysterical Heritage
now haveth its own book!"

From the wonderful whimsical world of the hugely successful
Hysterical Heritage greeting cards we present to you – *Panic Ye Not!*

The clever folks of Hysterical Heritage thought 'twas high time for
their cartoons to be enshrined into a book completely dedicated to
some old-fashioned medieval buffoonery. With more than 90 pages of
comedy gold and imagery inspired by the Bayeux Tapestry, this book is
a playful look at how our ancestors may have faced some of the highs
and lows, excitements and mundanities of midlife.

The modern world is full of snags and glitches, and though some might
say that these are merely first-world problems, we understand that they
feel as though they are tales as old as time.

Panic Ye Not! takes a playful look at how our ancestors would have coped; we don't think that they'd have done so much differently to us, although they *did* have bows and arrows and all we've got are never ending health and safety regulations.

Invasions, plagues, and only bathing once a week are nothing compared to our current struggles; not having Wi-Fi reception, failing to order in time for next day delivery, or simply forgetting your mobile phone. Although our lives are centuries apart, one thing that we do still have in common is our unique sense of humour.

If you've ever thought that the world of today is an unfair, constant bombardment of noise and nuisance then find an escape within this book and watch our predecessors try to handle it – it'll make ye feel better.

Should have gonneth
to Specsavers.

"OMG...
did I leaveth the iron on?"

YE ANTIQUES ROADSHOW

"Is it an heirloom?"

"Nay, 'tis only a loom."

All hail ye,
the Ocado delivery!

"Lost again!
He always blames
ye faulty Sat Nav."

"For services in finding flour in
shops for ye breadmaking during
ye national lockdown."

"Behold! Tis Dad, ye king of DIY."

Ye middle age crisis?

"We advanceth towards the castle!"

"Ooh great!
I haveth National Trust membership.
10% offeth in the cafe!"

"Oh soddeth, no gluten-free
vegan options again!"

"Bringst me back something
from overseas?"

"Yea, verily fine wines,
runny cheeses & one
massive Toblerone."

27

"Couldst Lady Jocasta ask Lady Lucy to ask Lady Georgina to ask Lady Rachel to pass the Prosecco?"

"How did they getteth
planning permission?"

A pole danceth
for your birthday.

"Amazing news from home my lord,
you could'st be owed PPI!"

All hail ye Queen de Prosecco!

"Panic ye not! Finally
got some reception."

"Arise Sir Dad,
defender of the armchair
and keeper of the
remote control."

"Urgent news?
The French defeated?"

"Nay my lord, better!
Waitrose is opening in
the village."

"Does anyone knoweth
the Wi-Fi code?"

Officially half a sentry.

Let's party like it's 1099!

"All ye single wenches,
All ye single wenches."

"If thou liked it, thou
shouldst have put a
ring on it."

All hail,
ye king of putting
out the bins!

'Tis thy birthday.
Let's go clubbing!

"The French attack my queen!!"

"Can't they wait?
Countryfile is on ye telly."

"'Tis the last time I let you
organise date night."

"Not more drunketh
eBay shopping!"

"We advanceth to Canterbury!"

"Ooh fabulous! There's a lovely
garden centre just off the A28!"

"One attacker at a time please!"

"'Tis health and safety goneth mad."

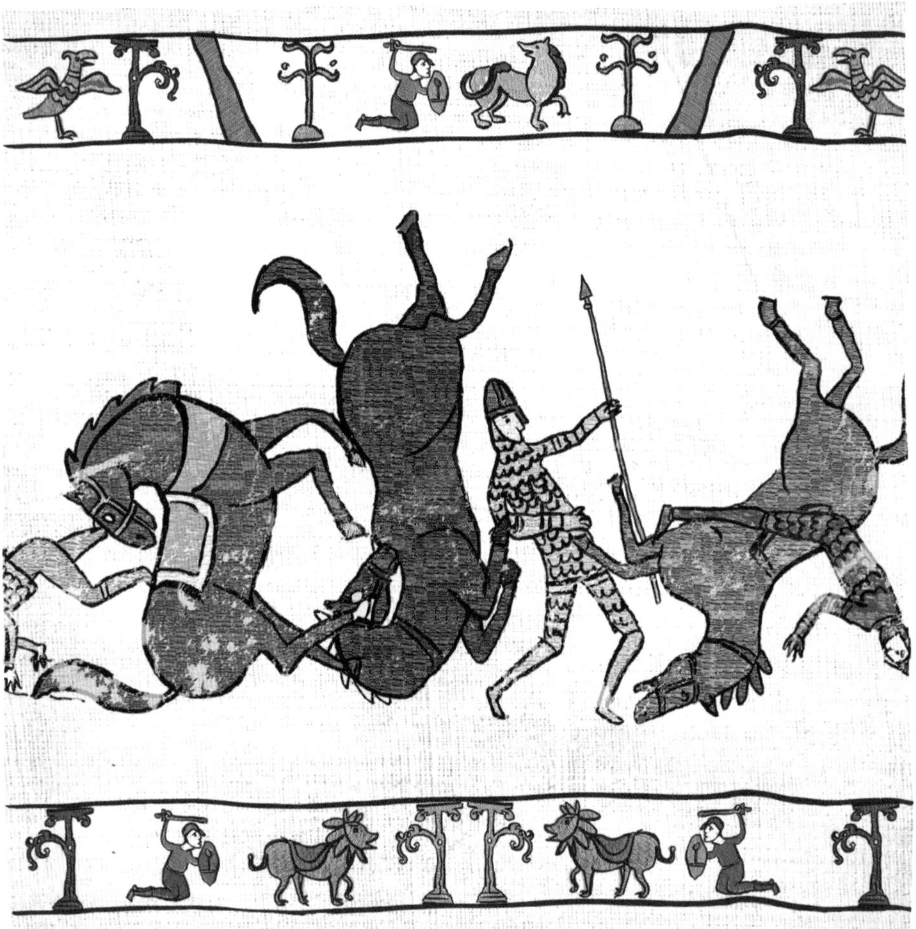

Hast thou been injured
in an accident at work?

"Stay strongeth!
The in-laws are coming
for your birthday."

"Tonight we feast with thy
cousins, my children."

"Haveth they got Wi-Fi?"

Ye perfect Christmas Dinner:
Ye sprouts from Brussels
Ye turkey from Turkey
Ye pudding from Iceland.

"Pulleth my finger, I fartum."

"Beholdeth the new
Apple 1-abacus."

William the conkerer.

We buy any cart.com.

"I ruleth this
conquered land!
Now bring me my
cup and Chaucer!"

Oneth Direction

vs

Taketh That.

84

Dunk & disorderly.

"Quick, the northerners are
arriving for Christmas...
hideth the silverware."

"Canst we just ask for directions
like any normal person?"

If you're happy and you
know it, clap your hands.

"Talketh to the hand 'cos
thy face listeneth not."

Acknowledgements

Ian Blake would like to thank in no particular order:
Lisa Hunt, Alex Lowe, Marc Blake-Will, Simon Nevin, Esther,
Jack and Alfie Blake, the Studio and Team at Woodmansterne
Publications Ltd,. and of course, William The Conqueror himself.